D1614126

Surprising Facts About Being an

AIR FORCE AIRMAN

by Kristin J. Russo

Consultant:
Kurt Waeschle, Chief of Operations
Navy Region Northwest Fire and Emergency Services

CAPSTONE PRESS
a capstone imprint

Edge Books are published by Capstone Press,
1710 Roe Crest Drive, North Mankato, Minnesota 56003
www.mycapstone.com

Library of Congress Cataloging-in-Publication Data
Names: Russo, Kristin J., author.
Title: Surprising facts about being an Air Force airman / by Kristin J Russo.
Description: North Mankato, Minnesota : Edge Books, Capstone Press, [2018] |
   Series: What you didn't know about the U.S. military life | Includes
   bibliographical references and index. | Audience: Grades 4-6. | Audience:
   Ages 8-14.
Identifiers: LCCN 2017017290| ISBN 9781515774280 (library binding) | ISBN
   9781515774327 (ebook : pdf)
Subjects: LCSH: United States. Air Force--Juvenile literature. |
   Airmen--United States--Juvenile literature.
Classification: LCC UG633 .R846 2018 | DDC 358.40023/73--dc23
LC record available at https://lccn.loc.gov/2017017290

Editorial Credits
Nikki Ramsay, editor; Sara Radka, designer; Laura Manthe, production specialist

Photo Credits
Getty Images: Christina D. Ponte/US Air Force, 27, John Moore, 10, Scott Olson, 9, Stephen Chernin, 6, USAF,
14; Newscom: KRT, 13, U.S. Air Force/Sipa USA, cover, 7, USAF/ZUMAPRESS, 8, ZUMAPRESS/Andrew Lee/
Planet Pix, 23, ZUMAPRESS/Ken Murray, 17, ZUMAPRESS/Mark Richards, 25, ZUMAPRESS/Nadine Y. Barclay/
Planet Pix, 15, ZUMAPRESS/Ssgt. Marleah Robertson/Planet Pix, 19, ZUMAPRESS/Tony R. Ritter/U.S. Air Force,
20; Shutterstock: ChameleonsEye, 21 (bottom), Chris Parypa Photography, 5, Pamela Au, 11, Thomas Nord, 24,
Harvepino, 21 (top); Wikimedia: U.S. Air Force/Senior Airman Chris Willis, 29, U.S. Air Force/Senior Airman
Peter Reft, 28

Graphic elements by Book Buddy Media.

Printed in the United States of America.
010364F17

TABLE OF CONTENTS

In the Air and Beyond 5

Joining the Air Force 6

Training 12

Working in the Sky 18

Working on Land 22

Working as a Team 26

Glossary 30

Read More 31

Internet Sites 31

Index 32

The Air Force Thunderbirds pilots fly F-16 Fighting Falcons. The pilots perform about 30 different maneuvers during a show.

FACT The Air Force is the youngest of all the U.S. military branches. It was established by the National Security Act, which President Harry S. Truman signed into law in 1947.

IN THE AIR AND BEYOND

There is nothing like a good "roof stomp" to welcome a new Air Force commander. Airmen make a lot of noise when a new commander arrives on base. They stomp on the roof and rattle the windows and doors. This tradition is all in good fun.

While the Air Force may have its fun side, it is all business when it comes to combat and military duty. The Air Force works to protect the United States and its citizens. The mission of the U.S. Air Force is to "fly, fight, and win in air, space, and **cyberspace**."

Air Force pilots, or aviators, fly some of the fastest and most advanced aircraft in the military. They train for years to "earn their wings." The Air Force uses fighter jets, tankers, and helicopters. But did you know that some aviators "fly" without ever leaving the ground? The Air Force uses **satellites** and **drones** to succeed in their missions. The Air Force protects and defends the United States on land, in the sky, and beyond. With more than 300,000 airmen in service, there are many unique and surprising jobs to fill.

cyberspace—the online world of computer networks and the Internet

satellite—a spacecraft that circles Earth; satellites gather and send information

drone—an unmanned, remote-controlled aircraft

Chapter 1

JOINING THE AIR FORCE

REQUIREMENTS

Anyone who wants to enlist in the Air Force must be between 17 and 39 years old. Recruits must have a high school diploma or have taken some college courses. U.S. citizens and people from other countries who have moved to the United States legally are welcome to become Air Force airmen.

How to Enlist

Men and women who want to enlist meet with a recruiter. Recruiters help enlistees learn about the more than 200 possible career paths in the Air Force. There are jobs in many fields. These include health care, computers, **aviation**, and emergency teams. The recruiter will also explain where to go to take tests that measure fitness and other skills.

All recruits must take the Armed Services Vocational Battery test. This test determines what job a recruit will be given. Many people join the Air Force to become pilots, but there are many available jobs. People who score high in science may be able to work with computers, radar systems, and nuclear energy.

When airmen recite the Oath of Enlistment, they promise to support and defend the U.S. Constitution. They also promise to obey the orders of their superior officers and the president of the United States.

aviation— the science of building and flying aircraft

ATTEND THE AIR FORCE ACADEMY

The Air Force Academy is located in Colorado. Students need good grades and high test scores to get in. They also need to pass the Cadet Fitness Assessment (CFA). The CFA includes many different physical tests such as push-ups and a 1-mile (1.6-kilometer) run.

Students at the Air Force Academy are called cadets. There are about 4,000 cadets at the academy. This means there are about 1,000 students per class. Cadets become officers once they graduate. Many students are interested in aviation. Other students choose to focus on topics such as English or math. All cadets learn field combat and survival skills.

Air Force Academy cadets march in formation past the Cadet Chapel every day. Inside there are Protestant and Catholic chapels and Buddhist and Jewish temples.

Community Volunteer Service

All cadets must work in the community. Some cadets install fire alarms in local homes. Others plant and care for community gardens or distribute food at food banks. Some cadets take "alternative spring break" vacations. They travel to areas damaged by storms or natural disasters. They help to rebuild homes and businesses. From 2006 to 2016, cadets donated more than 30,000 hours of community service.

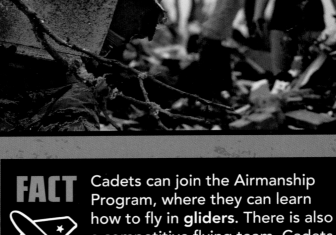

FACT Cadets can join the Airmanship Program, where they can learn how to fly in **gliders**. There is also a competitive flying team. Cadets can also "earn their parachute wings" by making five successful freefall parachute jumps.

glider—a lightweight aircraft that flies by floating and rising on

Not all officers have to attend the Air Force Academy. Officer candidates who have already earned a college degree can apply to Officer Candidate School (OCS) where they train to become officers.

When cadets graduate from the Air Force Academy, it is tradition to throw their caps into the air.

Officer Candidate School

Officer candidates report to Maxwell-Gunter Air Force Base in Montgomery, Alabama, for a nine-week training session. Candidates learn hand-to-hand combat and use different kinds of weapons. There is even a program on how to handle **culture shock** when they are stationed overseas. Officers graduate from OCS at the rank of second lieutenant.

Reserve Officers' Training Corp

Many high school students decide to join the Reserve Officers' Training Corp, or ROTC, when they attend college. In ROTC, they will take regular college courses as well as military classes. They will also learn to develop military leadership skills.

ROTC cadets attend formal military events while they are in college. They learn about military law, leadership, and management. They can join the Air Force as officers when they complete the ROTC program.

culture shock—the feeling of disorientation experienced by someone who is suddenly subjected to an unfamiliar culture, way of life, or set of attitudes

Chapter 2

TRAINING

BASIC TRAINING

Between 400 and 700 recruits report to Lackland Air Force Base in San Antonio, Texas, for basic training each week. Basic training is also known as boot camp. Training begins at 4:45 a.m. on the first day. Recruits go through eight and a half weeks of tough physical and mental training. A ceremonial march across the base marks the end of basic training. This march is called the Airman's Run.

Week Zero

Orientation is also known as Week Zero. During this time, recruits receive clothing and equipment and are assigned to dorm rooms. Male recruits are required to keep their hair very short. Their hair is cut three or four times in only eight weeks.

Weapons Training

Recruits are issued pistols and rifles. They are trained to identify the parts of these weapons and learn how to care for them and fire them. Marksmanship training is an important part of Air Force boot camp.

Survival and Emergency Response

Recruits learn what to do in a medical emergency and how to take care of one another on the battlefield. They learn how to stop bleeding from an open wound. They learn how to treat burns and broken bones. They also learn how to apply a **tourniquet**, help a choking victim, and manage a broken spine.

Airman's Challenge Coin

Airmen who complete basic training receive the Airman's Challenge Coin. The coin symbolizes that a recruit is ready to begin his or her career as an airman. It is a symbol of tradition and pride.

Recruits crawl through muddy obstacles during Basic Expeditionary Airman Skills Training (BEAST) at boot camp.

FACT To prepare for a career working overseas in different countries, recruits take classes in human relations and cultural sensitivity.

orientation—a program of introduction for newcomers to a college or other institution

tourniquet—a tight wrapping designed to prevent a major loss of blood from a wound

FLIGHT SCHOOL

The Air Force trains about 800 to 1,000 pilots each year. All Air Force pilots must be officers. Once an airman has achieved the rank of second lieutenant, he or she can try to earn a post as a pilot trainee. Pilot trainees must prove that they are pilot qualified.

U.S. Air Force F-16C jets can fly about 1,500 miles (2,400 km) per hour. They cost between $14 million and $18 million to build.

Pilot Qualified

To be pilot qualified, an airman must have vision that can reach 20/20 with eye glasses or with surgery. Pilot trainees must be able to see all colors clearly. Some people have problems with depth perception. This means they can see an object, but cannot tell how far away it is. Pilot trainees must not have any problems with their depth perception.

A person must be strong and fit to become pilot qualified. They must have a standing height between 64 and 77 inches (163 and 196 cm) and a sitting height between 34 and 40 inches (86 and 100 cm). Asthma and allergies will also keep a candidate from moving forward.

Simulators allow pilots to train without risk of injury.

Initial Flight Training

Pilot candidates who are accepted report to Initial Flight Training in Pueblo, Colorado. This is a 40-day test period where each pilot spends at least 25 hours practicing flying. Candidates must show that they can perform 20 basic flight maneuvers. Candidates who earn the highest scores in the Initial Flight Training program move on to a year-long program called Specialized Undergraduate Pilot Training.

FACT Usually, the military has very strict rules about wearing hats and saluting superior officers. Airmen follow a "no hat-no salute" policy around areas where planes are taking off and landing. This way they will not be distracted from the dangerous work at hand.

Specialized Undergraduate Pilot Training

Airmen who pass Initial Flight Training must learn certain terms and commands before they arrive at Specialized Undergraduate Pilot Training. This is so that they will know what to do in an emergency. If there is a cabin fire in flight, the pilot candidate must know what to do. If an airplane is losing fuel pressure, the pilot candidate must know how to fix it.

Training Challenges

One of the biggest challenges for airmen training to be pilots is handling high g-forces. G-force is a measure of the force of gravity. It is difficult for pilots to get used to the effect g-forces have on their bodies. Sometimes being in a fast-moving or spinning airplane will drain blood away from the pilot's head. This will cause the pilot to pass out.

The Air Force has a centrifuge where pilot trainees can practice feeling g-forces. The machine spins in the same way a spinning and diving airplane would. Trainees learn to clench their muscles to fight against the squeezing pressure of the g-forces. Pilots who are exposed to a lot of g-forces will wear special suits that inflate and keep blood from pooling in their feet and legs. This keeps them from passing out.

FACT  A new invention called the Automatic Ground Collision Avoidance System can save a pilot's life. If it senses that the aircraft is flying too low or is headed toward a collision, it pulls the plane back to the right course in less than 30 seconds.

An F-16 has a bubble-shaped covering over the cockpit. This gives the pilot a wider view all around. The seat-back angle is more comfortable for the pilot and helps with g-force tolerance.

Chapter 3

WORKING IN THE SKY

FIGHTER PILOTS

An average fighter pilot mission lasts between 6 and 12 hours. This includes time on the ground to prepare for the mission and to **debrief** afterward. Pilots bring snacks and water on board during long flights. They bring easy-to-eat foods such as protein bars. Small candies are avoided because they could get loose in the cockpit. Pilots must fly low enough to take their oxygen masks off so that they can eat or drink.

Call of Nature

Fighter jets and other small military aircraft do not have toilets on board. This can be difficult for pilots who cannot stop to visit a restroom when they're zooming through the sky.

If pilots stop drinking enough liquid it can be dangerous. Not drinking enough water can make it difficult for the pilot to concentrate and make the effects of g-forces feel worse. Holding urine too long can hurt the body.

Since 2008 Air Force pilots have used a new tool called a "piddle pack." A piddle pack is a special type of underwear that comes with a hose and a small pump. The pump drains urine into the bag. The packs allow pilots to fly for hours without having to stop.

debrief—to be asked a series of questions about a completed mission

The Air Force opened the role of combat pilot to women in 1993. Since then, there have been several female fighter pilots, including Christine Mau (above). Mau was the first female to pilot an F-35.

BOMBER PILOTS

There are only about 600 bomber pilots. Bomber pilots do not go out on many missions. Sometimes they fly just once a month. Bomber pilots fly jets such as the B-2 and the B-1B Lancer. A special design keeps the B-2 from being detected as it makes its way into enemy air space.

SPECIAL OPERATIONS WEATHER TEAMS

Weathermen in the Air Force are sometimes called "guerrilla weathermen." They make sure soldiers know what to expect about enemy territory before they arrive. Are there dangerous rivers? Maybe there are steep cliffs. Weathermen sometimes need to jump out of airplanes or climb mountains. They need to know how to hike through jungles and blow up obstacles in their way. Data is collected about many things, such as ocean tides, rivers, and snow levels. Other soldiers can then plan ahead before arriving to the area.

Airmen make High Altitude Low Opening jumps to avoid being seen by enemy forces when they enter unsafe areas. They wear oxygen masks so they can breathe during the free fall, which can be up to a minute long.

FACT In October 2016, Air Force Hurricane Hunters spent about 100 hours inside Hurricane Matthew, a Category 5 storm that moved from the Caribbean Islands to the coast of Florida. Thanks to information the Hurricane Hunters gave to meteorologists at the National Hurricane Center, 2.5 million people were **evacuated** from areas where Hurricane Matthew hit the hardest.

Hurricane Hunters

A hurricane is a large and violent storm that starts on the ocean. The winds travel in a circle. The center, called the "eye," is the calmest part of the storm. The Air Force Reserve's Hurricane Hunters chase storms. They fly directly into the hurricane's eye. Depending on the size of the hurricane, they might fly through about 300 miles (483 km) of strong winds to get to the center, and then face another 300 miles (483 km) of high winds to escape the storm on the other side. Hurricane Hunters collect information about the strength and direction of the storm. This way they can alert people who might be affected on land and at sea.

Hurricane Hunters drop a device called a dropsonde into the center of the hurricane. The dropsonde measures wind speed and wind direction as it falls through the storm. Hurricane Hunters share this information with other weather specialists. They work with them to predict where the storm will move next.

BOOM OPERATORS

In-flight refueling specialists are also known as "boom operators." They operate a "flying boom" that acts as a hose and will deliver the fuel to another plane in midair. This is tricky work and must be done quickly. Up to 6,000 pounds (2,721 kg) of fuel per minute is transferred from the fuel tanker to the target aircraft. Both the tanker and the airplane could be flying 300 miles (483 km) per hour. **Turbulence** could cause the boom to disconnect. If the boom operator does not act quickly, the aircraft or equipment could be badly damaged.

evacuate—to leave a dangerous place to go somewhere safer

turbulence—air moving unsteadily or violently

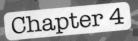

WORKING ON LAND

Not all airmen work in the air. Some airmen "fly" aircraft, such as drones and satellites, without ever leaving the ground. Other airmen take care of the many different types of aircraft used in the Air Force.

Drone Aviators

Drones are aircraft that fly without a human pilot on board. Drone pilots use remote controls from rooms that look like airplane cockpits. Most Air Force pilots are required to be officers, but the drone aviator program is now open to enlisted airmen. Drones take pictures of the areas they fly over to help the military gather information. Some drop weapons in bombing missions.

Explosive Ordnance Disposal

To work on the Air Force's bomb squad, specialists must be no shorter than 5 feet, 1 inch (154 cm). They also cannot be taller than 6 feet, 6 inches (182 cm). Members on the explosive ordnance disposal (EOD) team cannot be afraid of tight spaces. This is because the bombs they are sent to defuse could be in a small area. An EOD specialist knows many ways to defuse a bomb, but most of them are secret.

When EOD specialists are sent to different countries, they may use a "Packbot" to help them defuse bombs. A Packbot is a 50-pound (23-kg) robot that has wheels like a tank. It also has a camera and a long arm. The arm can be used to drag an injured soldier to safety.

There are many ways EOD specialists can protect themselves when they move in to defuse a bomb. Protective clothing and head gear are important to keeping EOD specialists safe.

Working in a Mountain

During the 1960s a bunker was built inside Cheyenne Mountain. This was during the **Cold War**. It was planned as a command center in case the United States ever came under nuclear attack. Today the facility is an Air Force base. About 1,000 airmen and civilians work there. There are 15 three-story buildings located deep inside the mountain. The buildings are built on top of giant springs. If there is an earthquake or a large explosion the buildings will bounce and sway, but not crack.

Airmen who work inside Cheyenne Mountain still monitor the skies to make sure the United States is safe from a nuclear attack or even a falling comet. If the United States is in danger, airmen inside Cheyenne Mountain will sound an alarm.

FACT There are two 23-ton (21-metric-ton) blast doors that lead inside Cheyenne Mountain. These doors are meant to protect the facility from a nuclear bomb blast. They are tested at least once per day to make sure they open and close properly.

Cold War—a long period of tension from the 1940s to the 1990s between Western democratic countries and Eastern communist countries

The blast doors at Cheyenne Mountain are made of low carbon steel, which makes them less likely to crack in an explosion. They are usually left open, but they were closed during the terrorist attacks against the United States on September 11, 2001.

Chapter 5

WORKING AS A TEAM

The Air Force was created to support the Army with a fleet of pilots for air combat. Its role has grown to provide support and protection to all other branches of the U.S. military.

Security Forces

The Air Force security forces act as police on military bases in the United States and overseas. They do everything from writing traffic tickets to protecting the base from outside attacks.

There are more airmen in the security forces than in any other field in the Air Force. Security forces members wear special blue hats, called berets. The emblem on the beret is a falcon over an airfield with the motto *Defensor Fortis*. It means "Defender of the Force." Security forces defend and protect military bases all over the world.

Combat Controllers

The combat control specialist's job is to help other soldiers fighting in faraway and unsafe areas. They join the Navy SEALs, the Army Rangers, and Marine Corps units on missions all over the world. When soldiers are low on ammunition or supplies, combat controllers will deliver what they need by air or by jeep. They scuba dive, parachute, and snowmobile to any areas where their help is needed.

Like combat controllers, combat rescue officers are special operations forces. They work with helicopter pilots to organize medical evacuations for injured personnel in all branches of the U.S. military and its allies.

FACT The Air Force was once a part of the Army. It became its own branch of the military on the same day the Central Intelligence Agency (CIA) was created. The Air Force has a long tradition of working with branches of the U.S. Armed Forces.

An airman trained to work with water systems helps the City of Hope. Workers at this Project Hope site provide help to children with cancer.

Project Hope

The Air Force and the Navy work together on a mission called Project Hope. They help victims of natural disasters. Since 2009, they've given about $33 million in medicine and medical supplies to more than 820,000 people.

Critical Care Support Teams

The Critical Care Air Transport Team (CCATT) is made up of three people. It includes a doctor, a critical care nurse, and a **respiratory** technician. They take care of patients in life-and-death situations. CCATTs travel on aircraft that are sent to rescue people who are hurt. They can begin giving life-saving treatment right away. They help soldiers injured in combat and take care of people hurt in natural disasters.

respiratory—related to the process of breathing

GLOSSARY

aviation (ay-vee-AY-shuhn)— the science of building and flying aircraft

Cold War (KOLD WAR)—a long period of tension from the 1940s to the 1990s between Western democratic countries and Eastern communist countries

culture shock (KUHL-chuhr SHOK)—the feeling of disorientation experienced by someone who is suddenly subjected to an unfamiliar culture, way of life, or set of attitudes

cyberspace (SY-buhr-SPAYSS)—the online world of computer networks and the Internet

debrief (dee-BREEF)—to be asked a series of questions about a completed mission

drone (DROHN)—an unmanned, remote-controlled aircraft

evacuate (i-VA-kyuh-wayt)—to leave a dangerous place to go somewhere safer

glider (GLYE-dur)—a lightweight aircraft that flies by floating and rising on air currents instead of by engine power

orientation (or-ee-uhn-TAY-shun)—a program of introduction for newcomers to a college or other institution

respiratory (RESS-pi-ruh-tor-ee)—related to the process of breathing

satellite (SAT-uh-lite)—a spacecraft that circles Earth; satellites gather and send information

tourniquet (TUR-nuh-ket)—a tight wrapping designed to prevent a major loss of blood from a wound

turbulence (TUR-byoo-luns)—air moving unsteadily or violently

READ MORE

Green, Michael. *The United States Air Force.* U.S. Military Forces. North Mankato, Minn.: Capstone Press, 2013.

Phillips, Melissa. *Careers in the U.S. Air Force.* Military Careers. San Diego, Calif.: ReferencePoint Press, 2015.

Simons, Lisa M. Bolt. *U.S. Air Force by the Numbers.* Military by the Numbers. North Mankato, Minn.: Capstone, 2014.

Whiting, Jim. *Air Force Special Operations Command.* U.S. Special Forces. Mankato, Minn.: Creative Education, 2015.

INTERNET SITES

Use FactHound to find Internet sites related to this book.

Visit *www.facthound.com*

Just type in 9781515774280 and go.

Check out projects, games and lots more at
www.capstonekids.com

INDEX

aircraft, 5, 16, 18, 21, 22, 29
    drones, 5, 22
    gliders, 9
    helicopters, 5
    jets, 5, 18, 19
Air Force Academy, 8, 10
Airman's Challenge Coin, 12

basic training, 12
boom operators, 21
boot camp. *See* basic training

Cheyenne Mountain, 24

explosive ordnance disposal
    (EOD) specialists, 22

flight school, 14–17

g-forces, 16, 18

Hurricane Hunters, 20, 21

Officer Candidate School
    (OCS), 10, 11

pilots, 5, 6, 14, 15, 16, 18, 22, 26
    bomber pilots, 19
    drone aviators, 22
    fighter pilots, 18
Project Hope, 29

recruiters, 6
Reserve Officers' Training
    Corp (ROTC), 11

weapons, 11, 12, 22
weathermen, 20